This Book Belong To:

_____

_____

Copyright @ 2023 by Star Dust
Dream
Published July, 2023
Manufactured in the United States
of America

www.prgarcia1.com

All rights reserved. No part of this book may be reproduced, transmitted, or distributed in form or by any means without the prior written permission of the publisher. This included photocopying, recording or any other form of electronic or mechanical equipment. To obtain authorization contact the author.

Illustrated by Pamela Garcia

Thank you for choosing *Tea Pot Wonderland: Fairy Homes Coloring Book.*

Coloring pictures is an enjoyable and accessible activity that offers a range of benefits for individuals of all ages and skill levels. Whether you are seeking stress relief, a creative outlet, or a moment of mindfulness, this practice can help you find balance and tranquility in your daily life. Witnessing the transformation of a blank page into a vibrant work of art can boost your self-confidence and self-esteem. It provides a tangible result that you can be proud of, regardless of your artistic background

There is no right or wrong way to color illustrations. Use your imagination. Try a variety of tools — colored pencils, markers, pens, pastels, and crayons. If you use markers or pens, place a piece of cardboard or heavy paper so your coloring does not bleed onto the next page. The pictures appear only on one side of the paper to help with bleeding. It also allows you to remove a page for framing, if you wish. There I a page where you can experiment with mixing colors.

The fact that you have chosen to support my work warms my heart. I hope the book brings you as many hours of joy as designing it did for me. Know that these pictures were a labor of love. I am thrilled to know they have found a good home with you.

Grab a cup of coffee or tea, sit down, relax, and have fun. You deserve some quiet time.

Thank you again for your support

Color Sampler

Not sure what color to use? Try it here or try mixing colors together

Congratulations. You've finished coloring all those adorable Fairy Tea Pot Homes. I hope you had fun. If you enjoyed the experience, please leave me a review on Amazon.

To view more of my coloring books, please visit www.prgarcia1.com. Sign up for my newsletter and receive free coloring pages, coloring tips, and notification of upcoming releases.

Never forget to have a little fun every day. Spred goodwill throughout your world. And keep your eye out for one of those fairy houses. You never know when you might stumble across one.

Additional coloring books available.

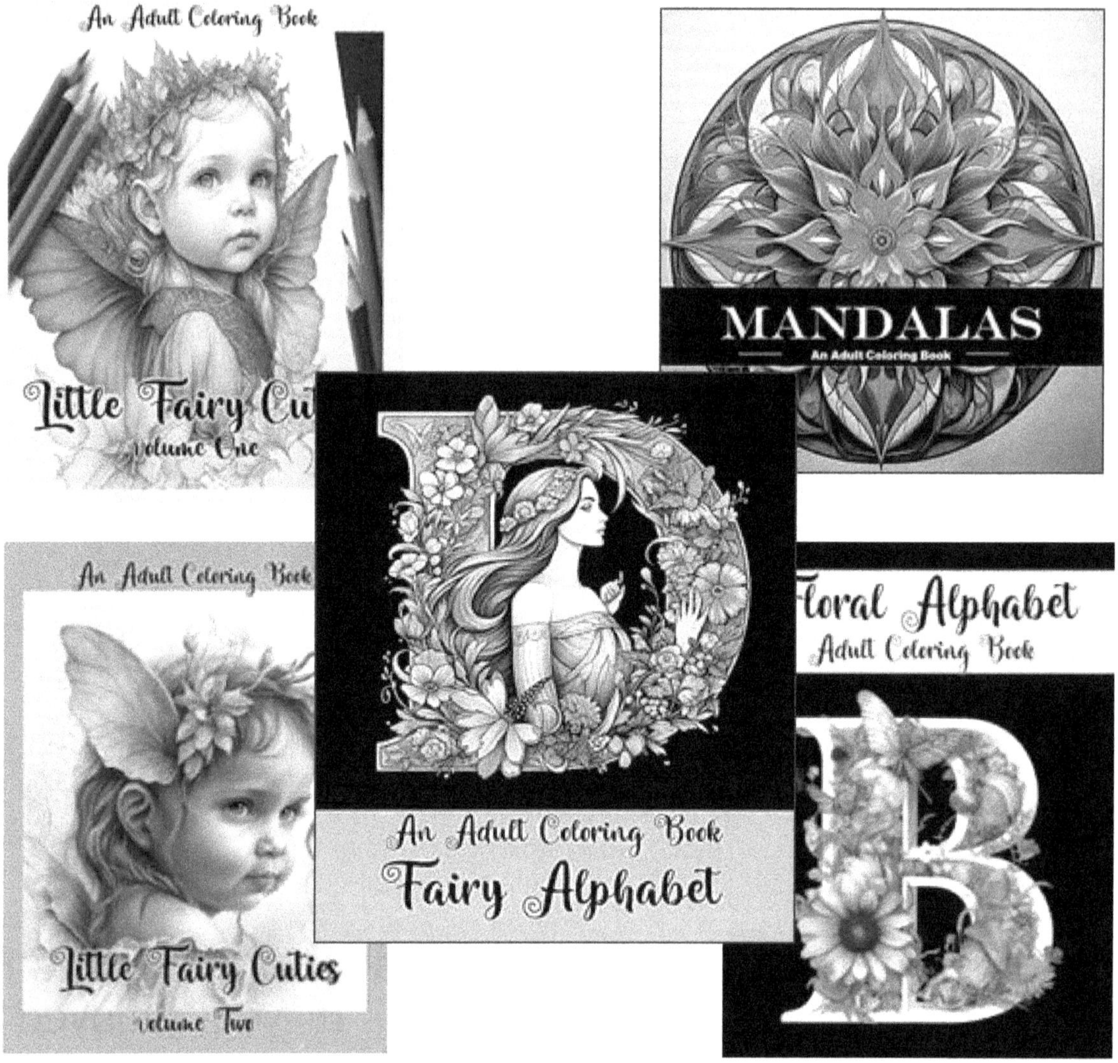

Please leave a review on Amazon

http:://www.prgarcia1.com

www.ingramcontent.com/pod-product-compliance
Lightning Source LLC
Chambersburg PA
CBHW081948070426
42453CB00014BA/2396